CW01501440

The Ritual of Enderi:
The Elven Middle-Days

By Calantirniel and Nathan Elwin

Elven Spirituality Press
United States of America

The Ritual of Enderi: The Elven Middle-Days

Copyright ©2016, 2017 by Calantirniel and Nathan Elwin. All rights reserved.
Published by Lisa Allen MH and Elven Spirituality Press
Interior Design by Lisa Allen MH and Art of Pop
Cover Design by Lisa Allen MH
Editing by Art of Pop
Tengwar Font Images by Dan Smith, edited by Art of Pop
ISBN#: 978-1549691683
10 9 8 7 6 5 4 3 2 1
Spirituality, Self-Help, New Age, Metaphysical, Body-Mind-Spirit

Limited **Print Paperback Edition License Notes:**
No part of this book may be reproduced in any written, electronic, recording or photocopying without written permission of the publisher, or authors. The exception would be in case of brief quotations, embodied in the critical articles, or reviews, in alignment with the Fair Use Act, and pages where permission is specifically granted by the publisher, or authors.

~~~

Table of Contents

Table of Images

~~~

Special Thanks

Along with Nathan Elwin, Calantirniel wishes to thank the following people who are very special, and dear to this continuing work:

Alyras de Cygne, current founding member and writing, editing, and musical contributor to Tië eldaliéva, and whom many of you may recognize as "Iluvamil". Your time and dedication are admirable.

Earendil Spindelilus, and Llefyn Mallwen, also current / founding members, and Adam Hayden, an original founding member: your presence is so much appreciated.

Ellenar, a contributor to Nathan Elwin's group, who in large part created the Elven Directions reference document. We love your unique viewpoint.

Luthien, and Eruannlass, also important members of Nathan Elwin's group: your contributions have been an important development of this path.

Dr. Markus Altena Davidsen, who opted to study all of us in-depth for his groundbreaking thesis in alternative religious studies, and even for the creation of this Glossary. Your work is so very important to the world!

Dr. Lance Strate, Media Ecologist at Fordham University in New York, USA, who wrote with the help of Rodger Ashton Smith in New Zealand, a beautiful poem about our beginnings.

Professor JRR Tolkien, his son, Christopher Tolkien, and the continuing Tolkien Estate (now titled Middle-Earth Enterprises Ltd.), without whom none of this would be possible.

Ray Allen, Calantirniel's husband, amongst many things, was a life-long Tolkien enthusiast who introduced the Silmarillion to her in the Spring of 2005, and who quickly passed the veil into the Blessed Realm in the Autumn of 2012 – you are so loved and so very missed. And?

You, dear reader! May this allow you to discover your own deeper access to the Elven viewpoint of Professor JRR Tolkien's amazing Middle-Earth stories.

~~~

Introduction

Tië Eldaliéva, meaning the Elven Spiritual Path, was founded officially in August of 2005, because a handful of readers of Professor J.R.R. Tolkien's Middle-Earth stories ("Legendarium") sprinkled around the globe felt there was much more present than well-crafted fiction, and in particular, with the post-humously publishings like *The Silmarillion* as they described the origin stories from the viewpoint of the Elves. True, the stories capture the imaginations of many, and the underlying themes happen to have a deeply moral, ethical quality. It is no wonder many spiritual seekers would compare the story themes with important aspects of their chosen path, Christian or otherwise. A casual book search online will reveal many book titles comparing the essence of Tolkien's work with those of their chosen doctrine (i.e. the Bible), or from nature.

But was it possible to implement only the content of Tolkien's stories, without comparison to other spiritual materials, and, as much as possible, follow a spiritual path based solely on the Middle-Earth stories themselves?

Two of the original founders, Calantirniel and Nathan Elwin, had deeply collaborated for hours (via telephone) to create, a workable, yearly *loa* (calendar) for its practitioners to pause, and to reconnect with the cosmology and annual energies, as well as to formalize the group's spiritual intentions, with the foundations Tolkien set forth in the Legendarium. With Calantirniel's ritual structure experience, (through her archetype familiarity, arising from her esoteric studies), combined with Nathan's immense knowledge base of the Legendarium, and his technical prowess for micro-sifting even the seemingly smallest detail, they painstakingly built, and at times rebuilt, the correspondences, so that the energies would never conflict with the Legendarium's material.

Before its sister community, Ilsaluntë Valion (the Silver Ship of the Valar), was established in 2007, Calantirniel and Nathan created a formal calendar, consisting of 21 rituals for the course of year. It is not claimed that these calendar correspondences are the only way to experience spiritual development on the Elven Path, (and Nathan proves this with his later work in Ilsaluntë Valion). However, these correspondences have proven in practice to be an excellent calendar that has been used, successfully, by Tië eldaliéva, for many years now.

In *The Silmarillion*, the first two chapters, entitled Ainulindalë and Valaquenta, describe in wonderful detail the Elven origin stories. Of note, there were 15 but later only 14 beings of "power" called the Valar, who are connected to Arda, our Earth. One of these 14 beings, the hunter Oromë, who had wandered Arda the most, is featured in this work for connecting with his energy and with the time of year for which the following ritual was created.

The Enderi ritual, presented in this work, was originally set by Tolkien, is part of Tië eldaliéva calendar, and is one of the path's most important workings. Enderi occurs every year between September 25-27th and are called the "Middle Days" because it lies exactly between Yestarë, the new year (March 28th) and Mettarë, the last day of the year (March 27th). It was a time of rest and travel for the Elves of Tolkien's Middle-Earth stories.

Appendix 1 features the complete Elven calendar year, so you can see how everything fits together. Appendix 2 provides you with a handy glossary to help with Elvish terms. The featured ritual is written for performing as a group. However, with easy pronoun replacements, this work translates quite well if you decide to do it for yourself. Enjoy, dear reader, the fruit of our wondrous labor!

~~~

Enderi, the Elven Middle-Days
(25th-27th September)

Honoring Oromë, who rides his horse while blowing his Horn

Chapter 1: "Lindë Elenlótë," The Song of the Starflower (to set the ritual circle energies)

Begin this in the center of the area in which you will be practicing ritual, facing East, (the direction of Origins/Cuivienen), while visualizing "mists" of swirling Gold, and Silver Light naturally "creating" ritual area – above, below, throughout the middle, and finally strengthened in the center, outward.

While toning - Hold your hands outward, and, when toning, then bring the hands together at the heart chakra, in the "Namaste" hand position, (which looks like prayer), if that feels right.

Tone: ERU

(Alternatively, you can tone "Ilúvë", the All/Everywhere, or "Ilúvatar", and/or "Ilúvamil", the All-Father, and/or All-Mother. The idea is to acknowledge, in a balanced way, the "All That Is". If you are Christian, you may wish to call instead upon the Christ Consciousness at this time, in your own way)

With your right hand, you will now trace a Septagram, (shown above, which represents the symbol of the Starflower), in front of you, while toning, as specified below:

(Approximate hand position, then tone aloud):

4:00: EL-EN-YA (Star Day)
8:00: A-NAR-YA (Sun Day)
2:00: I-SIL-YA (Moon Day)
7:00: AL-DU-YA (Tree's Day, for the Two Trees, Telperion and Laurelin)
12:00: ME-NEL-YA (Heaven's Day)
5:00: EÄR-EN -YA (Sea Day or Mariner's Day)
10:00: VA-LAR-YA (High-Day, Day of the Valar)
4:00 (Close): AR-DA (Earth)

To complete, and seal the energy, briefly form your right hand in the position of the "Fear Not" mudra, toward the center of the just-traced Septagram. This is done by simply facing your dominant hand's palm outward away from you, thumb and fingers up, extended and held together.

Now, tone: E – Ä (Behold!), while holding hands together at the heart chakra, then, going outward (the opposite of the beginning toning).

Chapter 2: Acknowledge the Directions, Call in the Valar, (and Acknowledge Ilúvatar)

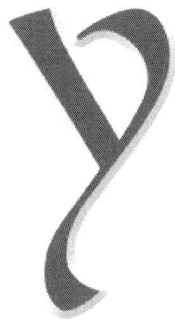

1. Go to, the East, trace the Tengwar for Romen (shown above). Open your hand into the "Fear Not" mudra, while intoning: RO-MEN (East). Leave your hand in the mudra, and say: "We now call on Manwë Súlimo, High King of Arda, of the Eagles, and Winds ... and his Lady, Varda Elentári, Queen of the Stars, and protector of Arda, and Ilúvatar's Children. We welcome you into our circle. Aiya!"

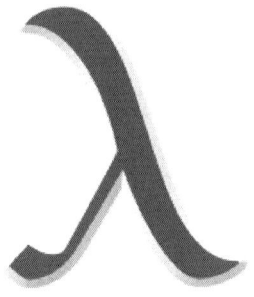

2. Go to, or face South, draw the Tengwar for Hyarmen (shown above). Open your hand into the "Fear Not" mudra, while intoning: HYAR-MEN (South). Leave your hand in the mudra, and say: "We now call on Tulkas, the youngest bare-handed ruddy Warrior Vala ... and Nessa, sister of Oromë, and friend of the deer; she who dances on new green grass. We welcome you to our circle. Aiya!"

3. Go to, or face North, draw the Tengwar for Formen (shown above). Open your hand into the "Fear Not" mudra, while intoning: FOR-MEN (North). Leave your hand in the mudra, and say: "We now call on Aulë, the Smith who dwells in the ground – the Vala of the mining, and crafting of metals, and gemstones – he who created the Dwarves as a gift to Ilúvatar ... and our motherly Yavanna Kementari, the Giver of Fruits, the Queenly Valië of Arda's maturing green vegetation of Harvest – and of LIFE that nourishes all of us. We welcome you into our circle. Aiya!"

4. Go to, or bring your concentration to the Center / Within. In whatever way feels right for your situation, draw the Tengwar for Óre, (Heart, Inner Mind, shown above). This could be in the center of your work area, or YOUR center, the Heart Chakra. Open your hand into the "Fear Not" mudra, (facing palm appropriately), while intoning: MI (Within). Leave your hand in the mudra, and say: "We now call on the Hunter Vala, Oromë, Lord of the Forests, he who loves the Elves, and wanders all of Arda on horseback with his Horn ... and Vána, the Ever-Young, and Vital – she who aligns with flowers, and new plant growth. We welcome you into our circle. Aiya!"

5. Next, face Upward / Above, and draw the Tengwar for Vilya (Sky, shown above). Open your hand into the "Fear Not" mudra, (facing palm upwards), while intoning: OR (Above). Leave your hand in the mudra, and say: "We now call on Lórien, the Vala of the high light Gardens, who nurtures our goals, visions, and dreams ... and Estë the Gentle, the Valië of Rest, Sleep, and Healing. We welcome you into our circle. Aiya!"

6. Next, face Downward / Below, and draw the Tengwar for Arda (Earth, shown above). Open your hand into the "Fear Not" mudra, (facing palm downwards), while intoning: UN-DO (Below). Leave your hand in the mudra, and say: "We now call on Those of the Valar Who Walk Alone – Ulmo, brother of Manwë, the powerful, and protective Vala of all of the musical Waters of Arda ... and Nienna, the Valië of our transformation, and rebirth – she who, with her tears, intensely cleanses, and restores all forms of fear, pain, and hurt that have come before. We welcome you to our circle. Aiya!"

7. Go to, or face West, the direction of the Destination of the Elves to the Blessed Realm. It is also ideal to have your altar in the West. Draw the Tengwar for Numen (shown above). Open your hand into the "Fear Not" mudra, while intoning: NU-MEN (West). Leave your hand in the mudra, and say: "We now call on Namo, the Vala of the balance, and fair judgment of our respective paths of Death ... and Vairë, The Weaver of the ever-changing black and white threads of Time – the Past, the Present, and the Future. We welcome you into our circle. Aiya!"

8. Finally, while continuing to face West, the direction of Endings, direct your concentration outward in all directions, and, in front of you, draw a FLAME, while intoning: IL-Ú-VË (The All, Everywhere). Form your hands into the Namaste mudra: palms and fingers together touching each other as if in prayer.

9. Say: "We acknowledge that we are One with Ilúvatar, (as well as the Spirit of Christ Consciousness)*, and feel the Flame Imperishable within us in our circle of celebration this (day/night)! Laita!"

*This phrase, in parentheses, can be implemented by Christians, and others to whom it feels right.

Chapter 3: Ritual

1. "LET US NOW CELEBRATE THE ELVEN MIDDLE DAYS, THE ENDERI, THIS DAY! Through the Legendarium, JRR Tolkien tells us that these three days were days of rest, recreational travel, and for being thankful for the abundance of the season. This "middle-time" is also considered the second of the three Fire Festivals, (the first being Tarnin Austa, and the third being Turuhalmë, i.e. the summer and winter solstices). These three days are dedicated to the hunter Vala, Oromë, the traveler to Middle-earth in the early times of the Elves. Though the Elves were more hunters than farmers, it is also a time of being thankful for the vegetation, whether fruit, vegetable, or grain.

At this turning of the Loa, (the Elven Year Calendar), Yávië the Autumn Harvest, is leaving, and Quellë, the Fading Season, or "Lasse-lanta" (Leaf-fall) has arrived. This also foretells of Hrívë, the Winter, to come. We, however, welcome the swift coming of the darkness, as we will be able to see more of the nighttime skies, including Isil, the Moon, (steered by the Maia, Tilion), and Varda's stars, while Anar, (the Sun steered by the Maia, Arien), is directed toward the shortening hours of Arda's presence, for a time to later return. Let us now reflect on this meaning, and the spiritual application it has in our lives on this plane of Earth existence! Let us also be restful, and thankful for the seeds of our goals, planted during Coirë, the Stirring Season, and Tuilë, the Springtime, that have come forth in physical manifestation, as we turn our attentions now toward our spiritual growth! Laita!"

2. Prepare Water for Meditation. Infuse Starflower* Essence (or other appropriate flower essence) to prepare for spiritual work, by creating Starflower water to drink through your intention, or through the actual Flower Essence itself.
*The Starflower can be of any Genus/species, preferably white. (i.e. Trientalis spp.)

3. Meditation. If you can, drink water (Starflower-infused, or not). To infuse, either purchase the essence itself – or – look at a picture of a Starflower, and then, by intention, receive the flower energy into your body through your eyes, then transfer it to the water you will drink via your hands. This takes focus, but can be done. You may find another way to accomplish this; if so, go with it!
Now, get really comfortable, feet flat on the floor, and uncrossed, hands open/uncrossed, and facing up, or down, as you see fit.

Close your eyes, and notice you are standing on Corollairë, the Green Mound of the Two Trees. See the beautiful silvery moonlight of the White Tree, Telperion, fill the left side of your body while seeing your left side glow silver, and while seeing this light in your very blood. And especially circulate this silver light to your Ajna, or third eye chakra, as well as your sacral (orange) chakra, about 3 inches below your belly button. If you see other colors along with this silver light, that is fine. Allow...

Now, fill the right side of your body with the gorgeous golden sunlight of the Golden Tree, Laurelin, while seeing your right side glowing golden, and the golden light in your very blood. You may see other colors along with this golden light, too; if so, just allow, this is fine. Circulate this golden energy around, and see it in your blood. Also, direct this golden energy to your crown chakra (at top of your head), and your solar plexus (the soft-spot just below the joining of your ribcage). Allow yourself to be nurtured above by this healing light.

Next, feel your tree roots pushing deeper, and deeper into Arda, our Earth, and allow Arda to nurture, and nourish you, while you are feeling more grounded, and connected to Arda. You are feeling VERY supported by Arda now, and, in fact, you ARE Arda. You may see more colors; if so, they are fine. As you have extended roots with your feet, allow your arms, hands, fingers, and even your hair to become various branches of the Two Trees--and see yourself REACH to Vilya, the Sky, in all directions. As you extend branches, extend your roots further--"as above, so below." Remember that, in order for your branches to reach to the far spaces of Elven, and ancestral memory, it is best to be centered in the Source so you can go even further!

Now, just as the trees had a symbiotic relationship, see the silver light, then, the gold light, fluctuating within you in a beautifully balanced way, (in nature's ever-wise way, and the season's Flow.) At this point, you will probably feel connected to Eä, and Ilúvatar. You may also connect with the Valar, and/or your Maiar, or Elven guides at this point. You also may start getting some visions now, or messages of some sort. You may be more fully re-awakening your Elven DNA, and/or ancestral memory. Allow all these to take their respective courses before continuing with this meditation; (1-3 minutes or so).

Then, visualize yourself with the protective, hunting Vala, Oromë of the Forest, with Valaroma, his horn, riding Nahar, his white horse who shines silver at night. He may have hounds with him. He loves the Elves the most, and asks you to join him on his continuing, and widespread travels around Arda – showing you the waters of awakening, Cuiviénen, in the East, where the Elves first awakened, all the way Westward, throughout Arda, pausing occasionally to see all the beauty of nature, from the woods, to the seas. Feel his love, and utter compassion, and devotion to the Quendi, the Elves, as he sacrifices his very existence by extending his help to them. He may even take you briefly all the way Westward to Valinor, the Blessed Realm. If so, see the site of the Two Trees. Other guides may arrive in your meditation. Remember any symbols, or correspondences that are presented to you. Allow all the time you need for this to occur; (5-20 minute pause).

Chapter 4: Closing

When the time is right, your meditation can come to a close. Thank the Valar, especially Oromë, and your Maiar, or Elven guides, for their assistance, and slowly come back to the physical world, remembering what transpired! Bid Oromë, and any others farewell, then, turn your attention back.

Then, slowly to Corollairë, the Green Mound of the Two Trees, bringing your consciousness to the Trees themselves. Draw in your "branches" and as you do so, begin to "unroot" from Arda, realizing you always have this connection. Then, slow down the golden energy, then slow down the silver energy, until the energy becomes small and portable.

Keep a little piece of each of these "lights", and then visualize this combined light becoming the three Silmarils, the jewels made with the light of the Two Trees. You can keep these with you, even in your pocket, and you can access their healing energy any time you want!

Now – take a deep breath, and, if you are still "buzzed", that will go away when we do bread, and drink. You should be back by now, feeling very refreshed!

Chapter 5: Extend Final Acknowledgments, and Open the Circle

1. "Our work is done! We acknowledge the existence of Ilúvatar, (All that Is) and the Flame Imperishable, while we are in circle, (and, we thank the Christ Spirit for being with us in circle).* May we see your Presence in all outside this circle. Laita!"
This phrase, in parentheses, can be implemented by Christians, and others to whom it feels right.

2. "Thank you, to all of the Valar, and in particular to Oromë, for being with us in circle, and for carrying out, in Spirit, our work done here (today/tonight). We hereby open ourselves to you, even outside this circle. Laita!"

3. "We acknowledge, and are grateful to the Elements, and Directions, and to the Silver, and Golden Light, for creating our blessed space, in which we may do our spiritual work this sacred (day/night). Laita!"

4. (Next, we "push down" the gold/silver light "sphere" of energy downward toward Arda). "Arda, here is a gift of energy of pure intent of love, light, and healing that comes from the deepest places in our hearts. May it heal you, and all of your inhabitants, and bring all things to natural balance. The circle is open – Laita!" (Push it all the way until Arda absorbs the circle's light into the ground)

5. (Grounding with Music, Bread, and Drink – many different options here!) Here is a place where we can reflect alone or with others on our experiences in circle.

~~~

Appendix 1: Tië Eldaliéva's Yearly Calendar Correspondences

I. Solar Observances

The seven Feast Holidays, (according to Tolkien, aligned with Northern Hemisphere), plus one additional observance, improvised by Tië eldaliéva, and Ilsaluntë Valion.

March 28th – Vinya Loa ('New Year') (Yestarë) – Vairë (Also, the start of Tuilë, the Elven Spring)

May 22nd – Birth of Flowers (Nost-na-Lothion) – Vána (Also, the start of Lairë, the Elven Summer)

June 21st – The 'Gates of Summer' (Tarnin Austa) – Anar/Arien/Sun (Also, Summer Solstice)

August 2nd – Bringing Forth of Fruit/Harvest (Yávië) – Arda (Middle-earth) (Also, the start of Yávië, the Elven Autumn)

September 25th - 27th – Middle Days (Enderi) – Oromë (Also, the start of Quellë, the Elven Fading Season)

November 21st (Cuivérë Quendiva) – Elves (the Origin/Awakening celebration) (Also, the start of Hrivë, the Elven Winter) [Additional observance improvised by Tië eldaliéva, and Ilsaluntë Valion.]

December 21st – The Logdrawing (Turuhalmë) – Isil/Tilion/Moon (Also, Winter Solstice)

February 1st – The Purification (Sovalwaris) – Nienna (Also, the start of Coirë, the Elven Stirring Season)

II. Lunar Observances

The 13 Elven New Moons (Cueran) and the 13 Elven Full Moons (Isil), approximately April through March, (plus 13th New and Full Moon improvised by Tië eldaliéva). New and Full Moons are calculated specifically by the Calendar of Númenor here:

www.glyphweb.com/arda/dates.html

We then place the Gregorian Date of the New or Full Moon, determined on nearly any calendar. We reference the month, and if the same month repeats, we then determine the second one is Cueranmaiaron if new, Isilmaiaron if full. Please note that the "maiaron" moons very rarely if ever occur in the usual pairing pattern. If we ever need the day of the season, we instead use the Reckoning of the Rivendell Calendar.✴ ·

Cueranviressë / Isilviressë (Moon of Youth): Tulkas

Cueranlotessë / Isillotessë (Moon of Flowers): Nessa

Cuerannarië / Isilnarië (Moon of Bright Fire): Varda

Cuerancermië / Isilcermië (Moon of First Harvest): Irmo/Lórien

Cueranurimë / Isilurimë (Moon of Heat): Ainur (and mention of Flame Imperishable of Ilúvatar)

Cueranyavannië / Isilyavannië (Moon of Yavanna, Giver of Fruits): Yavanna

Cuerannarquelië / Isilnarquelië (Moon of Fiery Fading): Námo/Mandos

Cueranhisimë / Isilhisimë (Moon of Mists): Estë

Cueranringarë / Isilringarë (Moon of Frosty Cold): Mourning of the Dark One's mark on Eä/Arda**

Cuerannarvinyë / Isilnarvinyë (Moon of New Fire): Aulë

Cuerannenimë / Isilnenimë (Moon of Waters): Ulmo

Cueranmaiaron / Isilmaiaron (Moon of the Maiar): The Maiar, which include the Fae

*** *The Dark One is Melkor/Morgoth specifically, but these names are not used (as per Elven etiquette)*

~~~

Appendix 2: Glossary

Qu = Quenya, the old Elven language, or 'Elf-Latin.'
S = Sindarin, the language of the Elves in Middle-earth, at the time of The Lord of the Rings.

Arda. (Qu: Middle-Earth). The name of Earth from the Elves.

Aiya. (Qu: hail!). Exclamation used to great the Valar.

Blessed Realm, the. Aman, in Quenya. Also known as Valinor. The realm of the Valar, and the Elves, to the West. Accessible to humans only in death, or through the path of dreams.

Cirth. (S: runes). Writing system developed by the Elves in Middle-earth, but used mostly by the Dwarves. Not featured in this version of the ritual for simplicity. A free download featuring Cirth is available for those on the Email List at ElvenSpirituality.com. See also "Tengwar" below.

Cuiviénen. (Qu: awakening-water). The place, a lake where the Elves first awakened, and where they were found by Oromë.

Enderi. (Qu: middle-days). Three days added to calendar of the Elves Oromë, in Rivendell, in the middle of the year, between the seasons of Yávië (Autumn), and Quëlle (Fading). As the Elven year begins in late March, Enderi falls around 25-27 September.

Ilúvatar. (Qu: Father of All). The Creator, God, in Tolkien's cosmology (also called Eru).

Ilúvë. (Qu: the whole; the all). Particle in the name Ilúvatar. Used here to express a pantheistic conception of the divine.

Laita. (Qu: praise!). Tolkien only uses this term in composite nouns, such as the Erulaitalë (Qu: Praise to Eru), one of the great Númenórean festivals. The use of the term *laita*, in ritual, was introduced by Sandra Kynes, in her book, A Year of Ritual, 2004, Woodbury, MN: Llewellyn Publications.

Laurelin. (Qu: Song of gold). The younger of the Two Trees of Valinor, created by Yavanna. Source of golden light, before the creation of the Sun.

Maiar. Ainur (Holy Ones) of lower rank than the Valar. Gandalf belongs to the class of Maiar.

Oromë. (Qu: horn-blowing). One of the Valar, spouse of Vána. Lover of Middle-earth, and teacher of Elves, and humans.

Telperion. (Qu: Silver—). The elder of the Two Trees of Valinor, created by Yavanna. Source of silver light before the creation of the Moon.

Tengwar. (Qu: Letters). Elven writing system used for the Elven languages, Quenya, and Sindarin, and for many other languages in Middle-earth. Featured instead of Cirth in this version of the ritual for simplicity. See "Cirth" above.

Valar. (Qu: The Powers). The fourteen most powerful of those Ainur (Holy Ones), who entered the world after assisting Ilúvatar with its creation. The Valar are Manwë, Varda, Tulkas, Nessa, Aulë, Yavanna, Oromë, Vána, Lórien, Estë, Ulmo, Nienna, Namo [also called Mandos], and Vairë.

Calantirniel (USA – Southern California) is published in over two dozen annuals, through Llewellyn Worldwide Limited since 2007. She is also published through the small UK press, John Hunt Publishing/Moon Books with vignettes in *Paganism 101*, *Pagan Planet*, and the upcoming *Everyday Magic Book*. She has practiced many forms of Nature-based spirituality, for a quarter century, and is currently exploring her Irish roots. Professionally as Lisa Allen MH, she is an astrologer, herbalist, tarot card reader, event timing expert, dowser, reiki master, energy healer, ULC reverend, and flower essence creator/practitioner. She is also a co-founder of Tië eldaliéva, meaning the Elven Path, a spiritual practice based upon the Elves' viewpoint in JRR Tolkien's Middle-Earth stories, particularly The Silmarillion. Find her at **IntuitiveTiming.com**, and **ElvenSpirituality.com**.

Nathan Elwin (USA – Georgia) has been continually reading Tolkien's Middle-Earth stories, since childhood. In 1977, when Professor JRR Tolkien's posthumous publication, *The Silmarillion*, was published, its stories allowed him, at a young age, to naturally implement an ethical and moral center, even greatly contributing toward his personal spiritual belief, and practice (despite having been raised Lutheran). Along with exploring magical and shamanistic leanings, he held this worldview by himself for over two decades—until the Internet enabled him to find others with a similar worldview. In 2005, he connected with Calantirniel, and Tië eldaliéva was conceived. As other members entered, and the group evolved, it was clear there were two distinct pathworking styles. In 2007, Nathan's group amicably formed Ilsaluntë Valion, (the Silver Ship of the Valar), to facilitate the purpose of developing a complementary path to Tië eldaliéva. The two groups still work together, and independently, to this day. See **forum.westofwest.org** to learn more.

Notes:

N · Aulë : The Smith who dwells in the Ground Crafter of Gemstones.

Sky · Estë : The Gentle: The Valië of Rest, Sleep + Healing

C · Oromë: The Hunter, Lord of The Forests

Under Ulmo : Protector of Musical Waters

Sky : Lorien : Of The High Light Gardens Nurturer of Dreams

W · Namo : The Vala of Balance + Judgement

Under · Nienna : Transformation + Rebirth Restoration

S · Nessa : Friend of Deer, Dancer on Green Grass. Sister of Oromë

E · Manwë : High King of Arda, Eagles / winds.

S · Tulkas : Young warrior

C · Vana : The Ever-Young, Plants, Flowers, New plant growth

W · Vairë : The Weaver of The Threads of Time

E · Varda : (Elentari) Queen of Stars + Protector of Earth

N · Yavanna : Giver of Fruits, Nourishment, life.

Notes:

25015862R00025

Printed in Great Britain
by Amazon